MONSTER
MINI-BEASTS

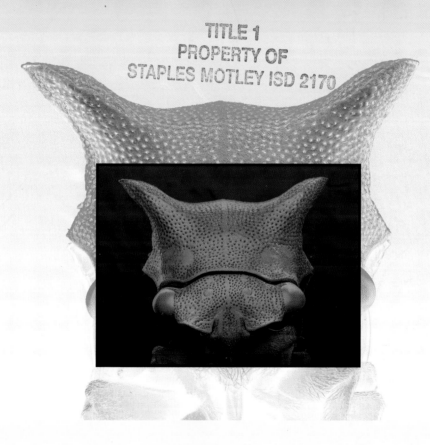

Jill Lewis

Revised USA Edition © 2003 Published by Scholastic Inc.
By arrangement with Reed International Books, Australia Pty Ltd.

Monster Mini-Beasts
0-439-64898-X

CSIRO Australia, Electron Microscopy Imaging and Analysis Facility/John Ward: cover, title page, pp. 6, 7, 9, 11, 15, 17, 19, 20, 21, 23, 25, 26, 27, 28, 29; International Photographic Library: pp. 4, 5.

Printed in China by QP International Ltd

10 9 8 7 6 5 4 3 2 1   04 05 06

Contents

Introduction   4

The Monster Back Swimmer   8

The Monster Water Boatman   10

The Monster Wood Borer   12

The Monster Leafhopper   14

The Monster Cockchafer Beetle   16

The Monster Bull Ant   18

The Monster Black Ant   20

The Monster Louse   22

The Monster Maggot   24

The Monster Elm Leaf Beetle   26

Microscope Monsters   29

Glossary   31

Index   32

Introduction

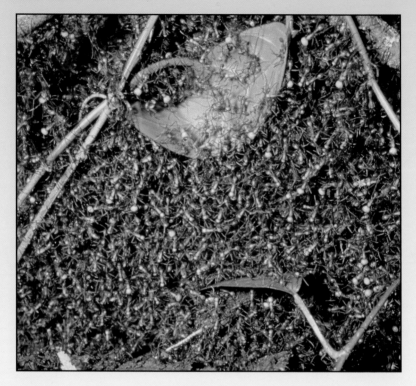

Insects can be held in the palm of your hand. But imagine if you met an insect that was bigger than you are. A monster mini-beast!

There are more insects than any other animal in the world, with over one million known species. They live on land, in water, and in the air. There is no place on earth that does not have some form of insect life. In their study of insects, entomologists are always discovering new species. No one knows how many insects there might be.

Even though there are over one million species of insects, they do have some things in common. Insects belong to a division of the animal kingdom called arthropods, which means "joint foot." All arthropods have three common characteristics:

- A hard external shell called an exoskeleton that protects the body of the insect. The exoskeleton is the insect's skeleton on the outside of its body. It works in the same way that a knight's suit of armor shielded him from injury.

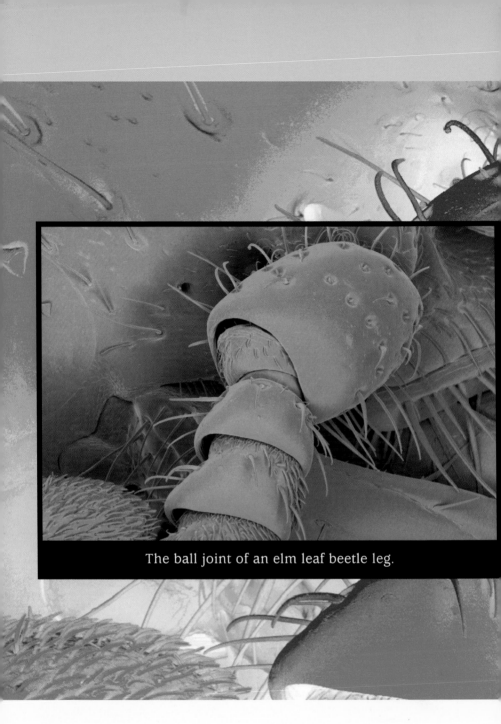

The ball joint of an elm leaf beetle leg.

- Jointed limbs. These limbs work like our elbows and knees. This joint movement is necessary to allow insects to move, in the same way that a knight's suit of armor had flexible parts to allow movement. Without these joints, when the knight tried to walk, he would have fallen flat on his face!
- A body that is divided into three parts:
  - The head holds the eyes, mouth parts, and a pair of antennae or feelers.
  - The thorax has three pairs of legs and one or two pairs of wings.
  - The abdomen has many segments, and contains the reproductive, excretory, and digestive organs.

The variety of insects' shape, size, and color is enormous, but we often don't know much specific detail about them because of their small size. The amazing photos in this book give us a closer look at these diverse creatures. The larger-than-life images show how insects are very well equipped to live in their different habitats.

The Monster
Back Swimmer

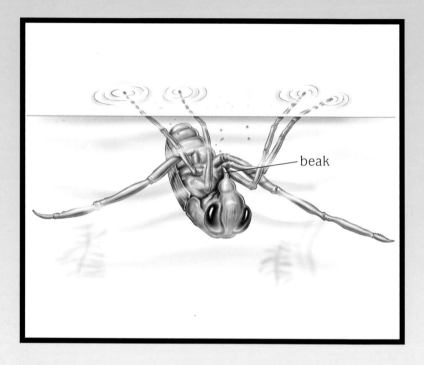

beak

You may see the back swimmer floating upside down on water with its long hind legs resting like oars, in a "v" position. The other two sets of legs, the forelegs and midlegs, are folded into the body.

The back swimmer is less than six tenths of an inch (15 millimeters) in length, with an oval head and an elongated, boat-shaped body. It has a strong beak to suck out the body fluids of tadpoles, mosquito larvae, and other small forms of water life. It is a fast-swimming predator and uses its forelegs to catch its prey.

The back swimmer is lighter than water, so it rises to the surface when it lets go of its hold on the bottom vegetation. The back swimmer cannot breathe under water, so it collects air bubbles on the surface. Its keel-shaped back has two grooves on either side of a central hollow, and a fringe of fine hairs traps the air bubbles there. Then the back swimmer dives down again in search of food. It uses its long hind legs for swimming.

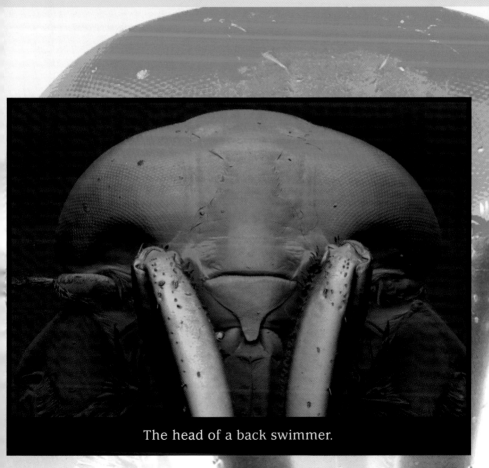

The head of a back swimmer.

The Monster Water Boatman

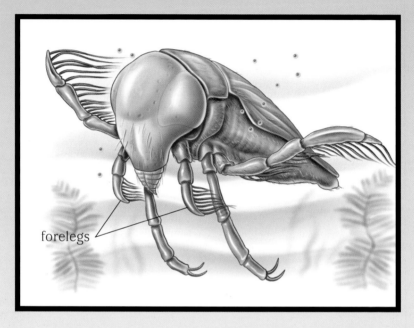

forelegs

The water boatman loves to swim on its back. This aquatic insect is often confused with another aquatic insect, the back swimmer. The water boatman, however, has a broader, flat, boat-shaped body, and a harder external shell. This insect uses its long, hair-fringed legs, which look like oars, to swim around with rapid, jerking movements. Its forelegs are shaped like spoons to collect algae and other small organisms for food.

Like the back swimmer, the water boatman conserves air around its body and under its wings so it can breathe underwater.

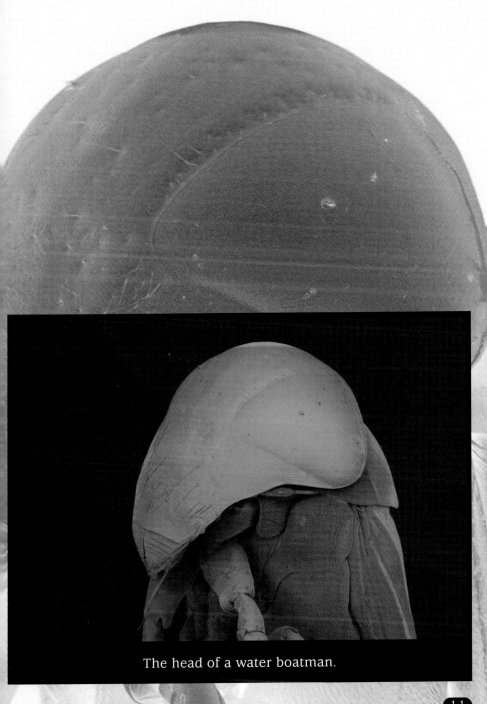

The head of a water boatman.

The Monster Wood Borer

This mini-monster can bring your house tumbling down
around you! It is a very destructive, tiny insect that
attacks and feeds on dry timber. There are two main
groups—the old house borer beetles and the
powderpost beetles. The female wood borer looks for
suitable wood in which to lay her eggs. The wood
pores, or openings, have to be just the right size for her
to insert the ovipositor, which is attached to her
abdomen. The wood must contain enough starch to
feed the larvae.

As the young grub grows, it chews tunnels through the wood, eating the starch in the timber. When it is ready to change into an adult beetle, it rests in a pupal chamber that it builds near the surface of the timber. Then it cuts its way through the wood, reducing it to a fine white powder. The wood borer will even chew through the plaster or timber lining of a house as it emerges out of its round, tiny hole.

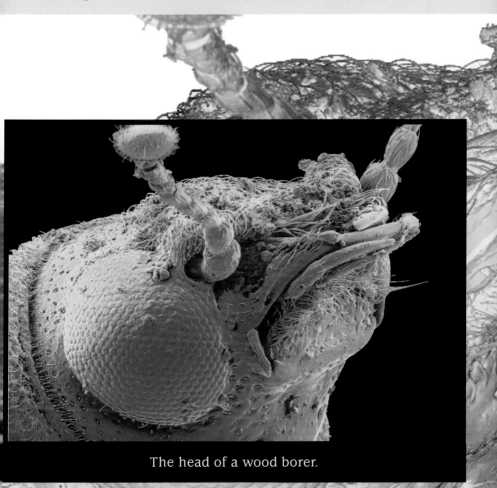

The head of a wood borer.

The Monster Leafhopper

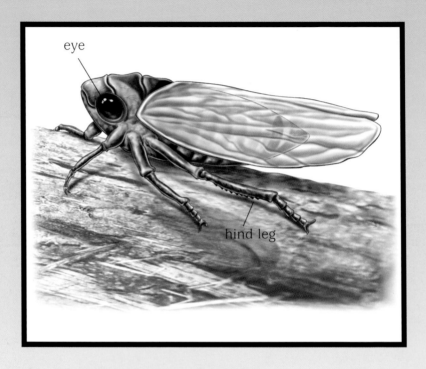

eye

hind leg

Insects are bilaterally symmetrical. This means that the left side is identical to the right side.

On the next page is the head of a small, slender, sap-sucking insect. The leafhopper has a torpedo-shaped body. Its mouth parts are fused into a long, pointed beak. The leafhopper eats a wide range of plants and leaves. Some species of leafhoppers carry plant diseases and are a danger for plants. Individual leafhoppers will not cause major damage, but large groups of the insect can be a problem.

The leafhopper produces a honeydew or sugary secretion that ants enjoy eating. Often, you will see ants near a community of leafhoppers, looking for a sweet meal. .

The leafhopper has long hind legs for jumping. It has good eyesight and reacts strongly to light. It is particularly attracted to lights at night.

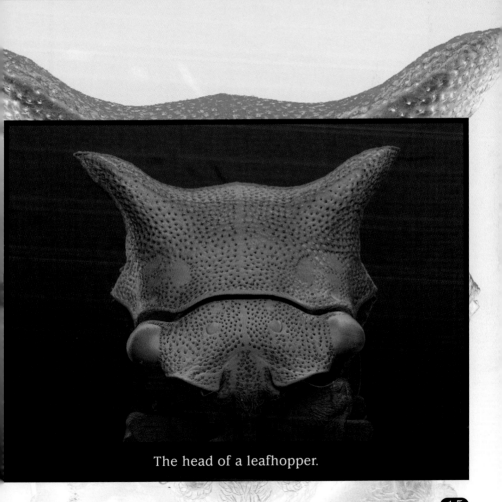

The head of a leafhopper.

The Monster Cockchafer Beetle

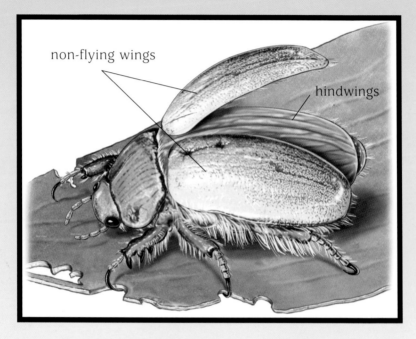

non-flying wings

hindwings

On a hot summer's night, this hard-headed little beetle will crash into the doors and walls of your house. But it rarely hurts itself. The cockchafer is a strong flyer, but it is also clumsy and noisy. It has to work hard to lift its squat, heavy body and sturdy, jointed legs off the ground. The cockchafer has two pairs of wings. The protective pair of non-flying wings covers the soft, delicate hindwings, which are used for flying. The cockchafer belongs to the insect order *Coleoptera*, which means "sheath wings." On the ground, the cockchafer walks around in a clumsy manner.

The cockchafer loves eating decaying vegetation or roots of grass. It burrows into the ground, using its strong head, which is formed of hardened tissue. The mouth parts are well developed for biting and chewing. The word "beetle" comes from the Old English word *bitula,* meaning "little biter."

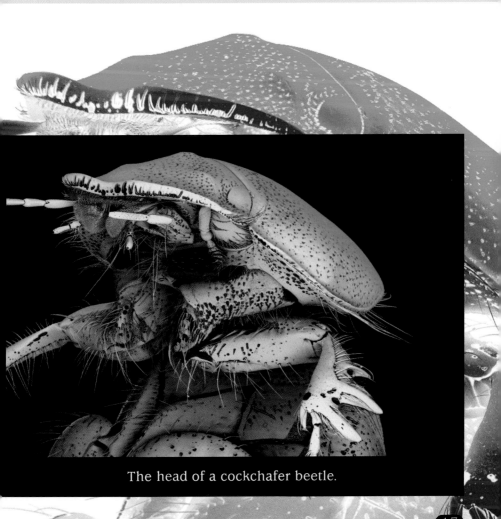

The head of a cockchafer beetle.

The Monster Bull Ant

Here is an insect that enjoys a good fight! The bull ant, native to Australia, has strong mandibles, which it can use to bite. The mandibles are the primary part of its mouth. They are hardened, strong-toothed jaws, which are used for catching and chewing prey. The mandibles move from side to side rather than up and down as our jaws do. The smaller pair of jaws inside the mouth parts is called the maxillae. This helps with further chewing of the food.

Bull ants will fiercely defend their nest and can inflict a painful sting on an attacker. The stinger is at the end of the abdomen. Ants are extremely strong insects and can carry and drag very heavy loads. The ant has a long body with a narrow joint between the head and the thorax, so the head can turn. The waist is very marked and defined. The legs are jointed and give great mobility and strength.

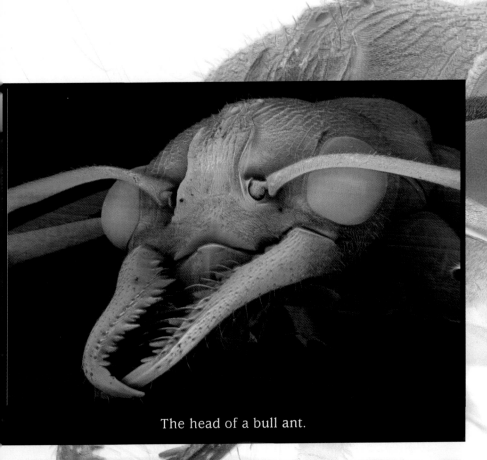

The head of a bull ant.

The Monster Black Ant

The head of a black ant.

When you see a trail of small black ants on the march to the sugar bowl in your kitchen, this is an army with a purpose. This is the face of a female worker in a colony of black ants. The worker has special roles to fulfill. It must search for food, feed the queen, and help to extend the nest. Ants are small, active, social insects that live in efficient, cooperative societies.

The antennae or feelers are one of the ant's major sensory organs. When ants meet each other, you will see their feelers moving in greeting. But they are also smelling and tasting each other. The antennae are angled with elbows for extra mobility.

The ant's compound eyes are made up of thousands of identical optical units, or simple lenses, which are placed closely together. In contrast, the human eye has only one lens. The lenses in the ant's eyes look like honeycomb. They are very sensitive to movement and light and give a wide-ranging view of the world. Insects' eyes are able to find different colors in their habitat.

The compound eye of a black ant.

The Monster Louse

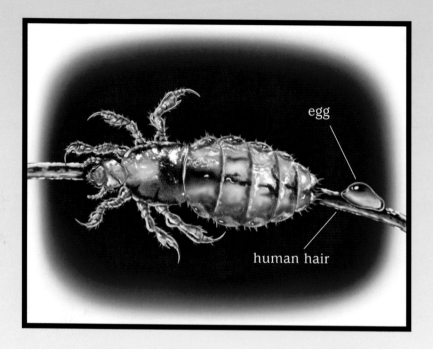

egg

human hair

This tiny insect would never live alone. The body louse is one of the most common sucking lice in the world, and is found wherever human beings live. This blood-sucking parasite uses the strong claws on its legs to find its way through human hair.

Over her lifetime, a female body louse will lay between 270 and 300 eggs. The eggs are incubated by the human host's body heat. Lice feed by breaking the skin and injecting saliva to extract the blood. This is what makes your skin itch.

When humans scratch the lice bites on their skin, the wounds can become infected with disease. The body lice carry the disease from one person to another. One of these diseases, epidemic typhus, has killed many people during wartime and in concentration camps, where conditions have been crowded and unhygienic.

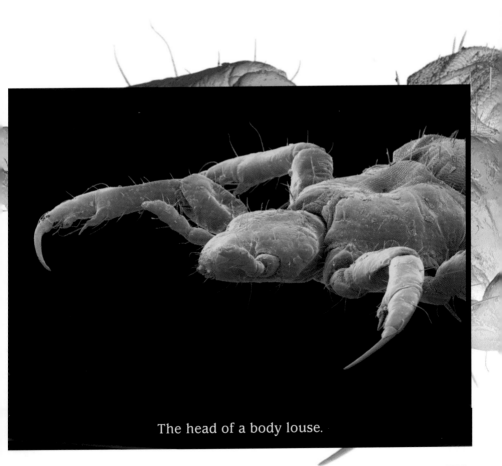

The head of a body louse.

The Monster Maggot

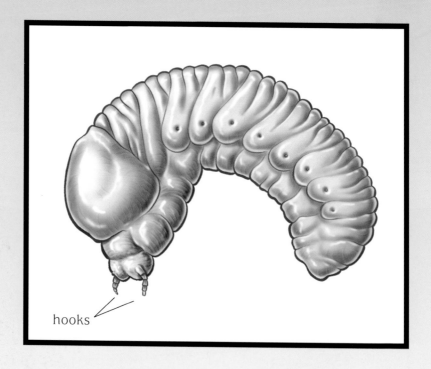

hooks

This little legless maggot can help solve a murder! The maggot is the larva of a fly. Forensic scientists have studied the stages of the life cycle or metamorphosis of the fly. Metamorphosis is the change in the appearance of an insect during its life cycle, from an egg to a sexually mature adult.

Forensic scientists know exactly how long each stage of the metamorphosis takes, from when the eggs are laid to when they develop into larvae or maggots and then later to the pupae stage, before growing into adult flies. They know that there are eight "waves" or stages in the maggot's life, which strictly follow each other over a certain period of time. So they are able to tell how long a corpse has been dead by the stage of the maggot which is attacking it.

The maggot's mouth parts has a pair of hooks that move up and down. Maggots love to eat decaying flesh, manure, or rotting vegetable matter.

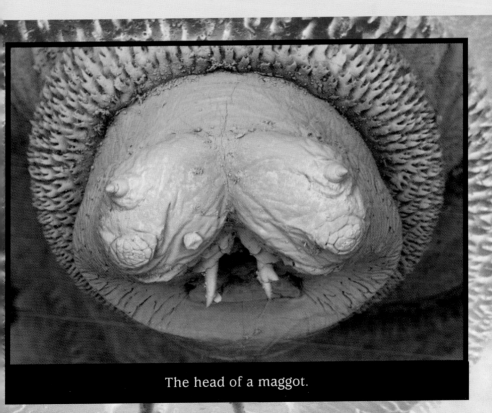

The head of a maggot.

The Monster Elm Leaf Beetle

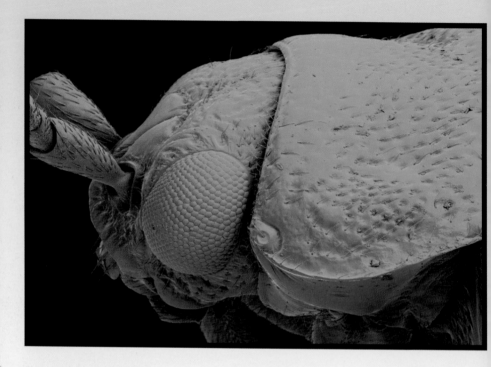

Beetles have biting jaws. They chew rather than suck their food. The upper lip, or labrum, helps to pull the leaf into the mouth. The elm leaf beetle lays her eggs on the underside of an elm leaf. When the larvae emerge, they chew the leaf until only the skeleton of the leaf is left.

Like the black ant, the elm leaf beetle has two well-developed compound eyes made up of a myriad of honeycomb units. Nerves carry information from the eyes to the brain.

Insects do not think before they act. Their behavior is a response to a certain touch, sound, sight, or smell. This response is usually a repeated pattern of behavior. Entomologists study the way an insect's sensory organs work, in order to understand insect behavior patterns.

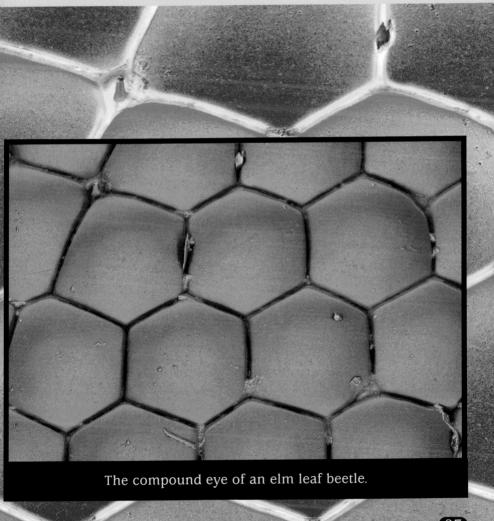

The compound eye of an elm leaf beetle.

The antennae or feelers of this wasp are covered with masses of tiny hairs. The antennae are a major sensory organ and are used for feeling and smelling. They are made up of different segments and can move in all directions.

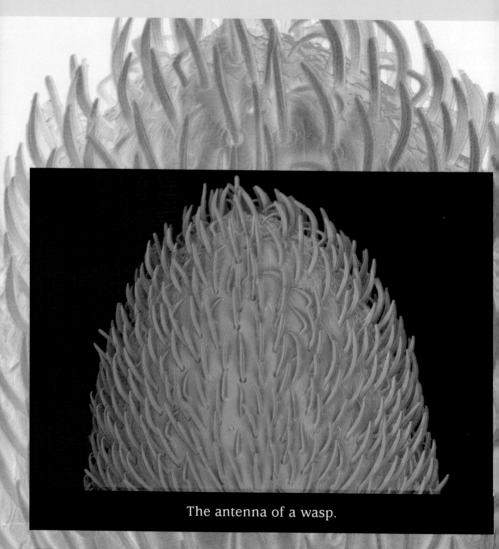

The antenna of a wasp.

Microscope Monsters

The monster mini-beasts in this book have been studied using a scanning electron microscope (SEM). The dead insect in each photo has been snap-frozen in liquid nitrogen. Then it has been coated with gold so that it will reflect the electrons from its surface as the microscope scans across it. The images can be magnified up to 100,000 times.

Scientists have developed the technique of adding color to the pictures from the scanning electron microscope. This shows the complex detail and diversity of the insect world, which you cannot see when you hold the insect in the palm of your hand. Viewing insects like this is a useful way of understanding more about the insect world.

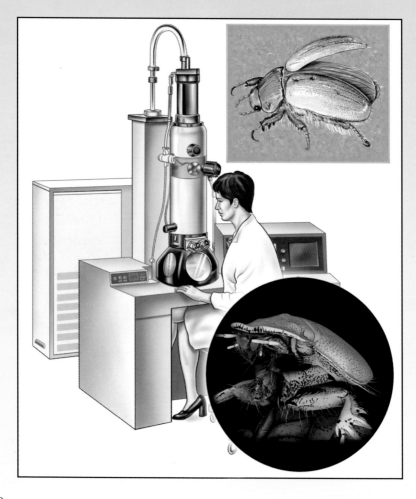

Glossary

abdomen — the rear of the three body divisions of an insect

diversity — variety; different forms or types

electron — a particle found in an atom, which carries electricity

elongate — to lengthen, make long

entomologist — a person who studies the forms and behavior of insects

excretory organ — the part of the body that discharges, or gets rid of, waste

forensic scientist — a person who uses scientific knowledge and techniques to investigate crime

incubate — to keep eggs warm in order for them to hatch

labrum — a plate or flap at the front of the insect's head, sometimes called the upper lip because it often partly covers the mouth parts

larva (plural: larvae) — an early stage in the development of an insect. It does not look like the adult that it will later become, e.g. a caterpillar, fly, or beetle

myriad — a great number, many

ovipositor — the part of the female insect's abdomen through which she lays her eggs

pupa (plural: pupae) — the stage in an insect's life between larva and adult when it develops inside a hard, protective case

thorax — the middle part of an insect's body, between the head and the abdomen, to which the wings and legs are attached

Index

abdomen 7, 12, 19
ant/ants 15, 19, 20, 21
antennae 7, 20, 28
arthropods 5
back swimmer 8, 9, 10
beak 8, 14
beetle 13, 16, 17
behavior 27
black ant/ants 20, 21, 26
body louse 22, 23
bull ant/ants 18, 19
cockchafer 16, 17
compound eye/eyes 21, 26, 27
corpse 25
decaying 17, 25
disease/diseases 14, 23
eggs 12, 22, 25, 26
elm leaf beetle 6, 26, 27
exoskeleton 5
eyes 7, 21, 26
feelers 7, 20, 28
fly/flies 24, 25
food 9, 10, 18, 20, 26
forelegs 8, 10
forensic scientists 24, 25
head 7, 8, 9, 11, 13, 15, 17,
    19, 20, 23, 25
honeydew 15
insect/insects 4, 5, 7, 10, 12,
    14, 16, 18, 19, 20, 21, 22,
    24, 27, 29, 30
jaws 18, 26
jointed limbs 7
labrum 26

larva/larvae 8, 12, 24, 25, 26
leaf/leaves 14, 26
leafhopper 14, 15
legs 7, 8, 9, 10, 15, 16, 19, 22
lice 22, 23
maggot/maggots 24, 25
mandibles 18
maxillae 18
metamorphosis 24, 25
midlegs 8
mouth 0parts 7, 14, 17, 18,
    25
nest 19, 20
ovipositor 12
parasite 22
plants 14
predator 8
prey 8, 18
pupae 25
queen 20
sap-sucking 14
scanning electron microscope
    29, 30
sensory organs 20, 27
social insects 20
sting 19
thorax 7, 19
timber 12, 13
wasp 28
water boatman 10, 11
wings 7, 10, 16
wood 12, 13
wood borer 12, 13
worker 20